Onion Rings

The Ultimate Onion Rings Cookbook

While every precaution has been taken in the preparation of this book, the publisher assumes no responsibility for errors or omissions, or for damages resulting from the use of the information contained herein.

ONION RINGS

First edition. December 19, 2023.

Copyright © 2023 Jose Maria.

ISBN: 979-8223194576

Written by Jose Maria.

Table of Contents

Jose Maria

❖ Introduction

A. Welcome to the World of Onion Rings

Welcome to the savory world of onion rings! This cookbook is your gateway to mastering the art of creating crispy, flavorful onion rings that will delight your taste buds and impress your friends and family. Whether you're a seasoned chef or a kitchen novice, get ready to embark on a delicious journey that celebrates the humble yet versatile onion.

B. History and Evolution of Onion Rings

Dive into the rich history of onion rings, exploring how this iconic snack has evolved over time. From its mysterious origins to becoming a beloved global treat, discover the cultural influences that have shaped the way we enjoy onion rings today. Gain insights into the various preparation methods and regional twists that have contributed to the diverse landscape of onion ring recipes.

C. Essential Ingredients and Tools

Before you heat up the oil and start slicing onions, familiarize yourself with the key ingredients and tools that will set the stage for onion ring success. From choosing the right onions to selecting the perfect batter components, we'll guide you through the essentials. Learn about the tools that will make your onion ring-making experience efficient and enjoyable, ensuring you have everything you need to create these crispy delights in your own kitchen.

Chapter (1) Mastering the Basics

A. Choosing the Right Onions

Selecting the right onions is crucial for achieving the perfect balance of sweetness and mildness in your onion rings. Consider using sweet onions such as Vidalia or Walla Walla for a milder flavor. Alternatively, yellow onions work well, offering a slightly stronger taste. Avoid using red onions, which can be too pungent for this classic snack.

B. Slicing Techniques for Perfect Rings

Achieve uniformity in your onion rings by mastering the art of slicing. Follow these steps for ideal rings:

- **Trim the Ends:** Cut off both ends of the onion and remove the outer skin.
- **Peel Gently:** Peel the onion, ensuring the inner layers remain intact for better ring formation.
- **Slice Evenly:** Use a sharp knife to cut the onion into 1/2-inch rings. Aim for consistency to ensure even cooking.

C. Creating the Ideal Batter

The key to crispy and flavorful onion rings lies in the perfect batter. Follow this simple recipe:

Classic Onion Ring Batter

Ingredients:

- 2 cups all-purpose flour
- 1 teaspoon baking powder
- 1/2 teaspoon salt
- 1/4 teaspoon black pepper
- 1 1/2 cups cold sparkling water or beer (lager works well)

Instructions:

Prepare Dry Ingredients:

In a large mixing bowl, whisk together the flour, baking powder, salt, and black pepper.

Incorporate Liquid:

Gradually add the cold sparkling water or beer to the dry ingredients, whisking continuously until you achieve a smooth batter. The bubbles in sparkling water contribute to the light and crispy texture.

Let It Rest:

Allow the batter to rest for 15-20 minutes. This allows the flour to absorb the liquid, resulting in a thicker and stickier consistency.

Now, you're ready to dip your perfectly sliced onions into the batter and create classic, crispy onion rings.

Chapter (2) Classic Onion Ring Recipes

A. Traditional Beer-Battered Onion Rings
   Ingredients:

- 1 batch of Classic Onion Ring Batter (see Mastering the Basics, Section C)
- 2 large onions, sliced into 1/2-inch rings
- Vegetable oil, for frying
- Salt, to taste

Instructions:

- **Preheat Oil:**

Fill a deep fryer or a large, heavy pot with vegetable oil. Heat it to 375°F (190°C).

- **Dip in Batter:**

Dip each onion ring into the prepared classic batter, ensuring it's well-coated.

- **Fry to Perfection:**

Carefully place the battered rings into the hot oil, frying in batches to avoid overcrowding. Fry until golden brown and crispy, approximately 2-3 minutes per side.

- **Drain and Season:**

Use a slotted spoon to remove the onion rings from the oil and place them on a paper towel-lined plate. Season with salt immediately while they're still hot.

- **Serve Warm:**

Enjoy these classic beer-battered onion rings while they're warm and crispy. Serve with your favorite dipping sauce.

B. Crispy Panko-Crusted Onion Rings
Ingredients:

- 2 large onions, sliced into 1/2-inch rings
- 1 cup all-purpose flour
- 2 eggs, beaten
- 2 cups Panko breadcrumbs
- Salt and pepper, to taste
- Vegetable oil, for frying

Instructions:

- **Prepare Breading Station:**

Set up three shallow dishes. Place flour in one, beaten eggs in another, and Panko breadcrumbs in the third.

- **Coat in Flour:**

Dredge each onion ring in the flour, ensuring an even coating.

- **Dip in Egg:**

Dip the floured ring into the beaten eggs, covering it completely.

- **Coat with Panko:**

Roll the egg-coated ring in the Panko breadcrumbs, pressing gently to adhere the crumbs.

- **Fry to Golden Perfection:**

Heat vegetable oil to 375°F (190°C). Fry the rings until they achieve a golden brown color, about 2 minutes per side.

- **Drain and Season:**

Use a slotted spoon to remove the onion rings from the oil. Place them on a paper towel-lined plate, and season with salt and pepper.

- **Serve and Enjoy:**

These crispy Panko-crusted onion rings are ready to be enjoyed. Serve with your preferred dipping sauce.

C. Buttermilk-Soaked Southern Style Onion Rings

Ingredients:

- 2 large onions, sliced into 1/2-inch rings
- 2 cups buttermilk
- 2 cups all-purpose flour
- 1 teaspoon garlic powder
- 1 teaspoon onion powder
- Salt and pepper, to taste
- Vegetable oil, for frying

Instructions:

- **Soak in Buttermilk:**

Place the sliced onions in a bowl and pour buttermilk over them. Allow them to soak for at least 30 minutes, or refrigerate overnight for enhanced flavor.

- **Prepare Coating:**

In a separate bowl, mix the flour, garlic powder, onion powder, salt, and pepper.

- **Coat in Flour Mixture:**

Remove each onion ring from the buttermilk, allowing excess liquid to drip off. Coat the rings in the flour mixture, ensuring an even and thick coating.

- **Fry to Southern Perfection:**

Heat vegetable oil to 350°F (175°C). Fry the rings until golden brown and crispy, approximately 3-4 minutes per side.

- **Drain and Serve:**

Use a slotted spoon to transfer the onion rings to a paper towel-lined plate. Allow them to drain and cool slightly before serving.

- **Southern-Style Delight:**

Indulge in the rich, Southern flavor of these buttermilk-soaked onion rings. Serve them alongside your favorite dipping sauces for a true taste of the South.

Chapter (3) Creative Variations

A. Spicy Jalapeño Onion Rings
Ingredients:

- 2 large onions, sliced into 1/2-inch rings
- 1 cup buttermilk
- 1 cup all-purpose flour
- 1 cup cornmeal
- 1 tablespoon smoked paprika
- 1 teaspoon cayenne pepper
- 2 jalapeños, thinly sliced (seeds removed for milder heat)
- Salt and pepper, to taste
- Vegetable oil, for frying

Instructions:

- **Prep the Onions:**

Soak the sliced onions in buttermilk for 30 minutes.

- **Create Spicy Coating:**

In a bowl, combine flour, cornmeal, smoked paprika, cayenne pepper, salt, and pepper.

- **Coat in Spicy Mixture:**

Remove the onions from buttermilk, allowing excess to drip off. Coat each ring in the spicy flour mixture, pressing jalapeño slices onto each ring.

- **Fry to Spicy Perfection:**

Heat vegetable oil to 350°F (175°C). Fry the rings until golden brown and crispy, approximately 3-4 minutes per side.

- **Drain and Serve:**

Use a slotted spoon to transfer the spicy jalapeño onion rings to a paper towel-lined plate. Serve hot with a cooling dipping sauce.

B. Parmesan and Herb-infused Onion Rings
Ingredients:

- **2 large onions, sliced into 1/2-inch rings**
- **1 cup buttermilk**
- **1 cup all-purpose flour**
- **1 cup grated Parmesan cheese**
- **1 tablespoon dried Italian herbs (basil, oregano, thyme)**
- **Salt and pepper, to taste**
- **Vegetable oil, for frying**

Instructions:

- **Prepare the Onions:**

Soak the sliced onions in buttermilk for 30 minutes.

- **Create Parmesan-Herb Coating:**

In a bowl, combine flour, grated Parmesan, dried herbs, salt, and pepper.

- **Coat in Parmesan Mixture:**

Remove the onions from buttermilk, allowing excess to drip off. Coat each ring in the Parmesan-herb flour mixture.

- **Fry to Flavorful Perfection:**

Heat vegetable oil to 350°F (175°C). Fry the rings until golden brown and crispy, approximately 3-4 minutes per side.

- **Drain and Serve:**

Use a slotted spoon to transfer the Parmesan and herb-infused onion rings to a paper towel-lined plate. Sprinkle with additional Parmesan and serve hot.

C. Bacon-Wrapped Onion Rings

Ingredients:

- 2 large onions, sliced into 1/2-inch rings
- 1 cup buttermilk
- 1 cup all-purpose flour
- 12 slices bacon
- Toothpicks
- Salt and pepper, to taste
- Vegetable oil, for frying

Instructions:

- **Prepare the Onions:**

Soak the sliced onions in buttermilk for 30 minutes.

- **Wrap in Bacon:**

Wrap each onion ring with a slice of bacon, securing the ends with toothpicks.

- **Create Coating:**

In a bowl, place flour, salt, and pepper.

- **Coat in Flour Mixture:**

Remove the bacon-wrapped onions from buttermilk, allowing excess to drip off. Coat each ring in the flour mixture.

- **Fry to Bacony Perfection:**

Heat vegetable oil to 350°F (175°C). Fry the bacon-wrapped rings until the bacon is crispy and the onions are golden brown, approximately 4-5 minutes per side.

- **Drain and Serve:**

Use a slotted spoon to transfer the bacon-wrapped onion rings to a paper towel-lined plate. Remove toothpicks before serving. Enjoy the savory combination of bacon and onion.

Chapter (4) International Flavors

A. Tempura Onion Rings (Japanese-inspired)
  Ingredients:

- 2 large onions, sliced into 1/2-inch rings
- 1 cup all-purpose flour
- 1 cup ice-cold water
- 1/4 cup cornstarch
- Vegetable oil, for frying
- Soy sauce, for dipping

Instructions:

- **Prepare the Onions:**

Slice the onions into 1/2-inch rings.

- **Create Tempura Batter:**

In a bowl, mix flour and cornstarch. Gradually whisk in ice-cold water until you achieve a smooth, thin batter.

- **Dip and Fry:**

Dip each onion ring into the tempura batter, coating it evenly. Fry in hot vegetable oil (350°F/175°C) until golden brown and crisp, about 2 minutes per side.

- **Drain and Serve:**

Use a slotted spoon to transfer the tempura onion rings to a paper towel-lined plate. Serve with soy sauce for dipping.

B. Curried Onion Rings (Indian-inspired)
Ingredients:

- 2 large onions, sliced into 1/2-inch rings
- 1 cup chickpea flour (besan)
- 1 tablespoon curry powder
- 1 teaspoon ground cumin
- 1/2 teaspoon turmeric
- Salt and pepper, to taste
- Water (as needed)
- Vegetable oil, for frying
- Mango chutney, for dipping

Instructions:

- **Prepare the Onions:**

Slice the onions into 1/2-inch rings.

- **Create Curry Coating:**

In a bowl, combine chickpea flour, curry powder, ground cumin, turmeric, salt, and pepper. Gradually add water to form a thick batter.

- **Coat and Fry:**

Dip each onion ring into the curry batter, ensuring it's well-coated. Fry in hot vegetable oil (350°F/175°C) until golden brown, approximately 3 minutes per side.

- **Drain and Serve:**

Use a slotted spoon to transfer the curried onion rings to a paper towel-lined plate. Serve with mango chutney for a delightful Indian-inspired twist.

C.   Churro-style   Cinnamon   Sugar   Onion   Rings (Mexican-inspired)

Ingredients:

- 2 large onions, sliced into 1/2-inch rings
- 1 cup all-purpose flour
- 1 teaspoon baking powder
- 1/2 teaspoon salt
- 1 cup milk
- Vegetable oil, for frying
- 1/2 cup sugar
- 1 teaspoon ground cinnamon

Instructions:

- **Prepare the Onions:**

Slice the onions into 1/2-inch rings.

- **Create Churro Coating:**

In a bowl, whisk together flour, baking powder, salt, and milk to form a smooth batter.

- **Fry to Golden Brown:**

Dip each onion ring into the batter, coating it evenly. Fry in hot vegetable oil (375°F/190°C) until golden brown, about 2-3 minutes per side.

- **Coat with Cinnamon Sugar:**

In a separate bowl, mix sugar and ground cinnamon. While the rings are still warm, roll them in the cinnamon sugar mixture to coat evenly.

- **Serve Warm:**

Enjoy these Mexican-inspired churro-style cinnamon sugar onion rings while they're warm and delightful.

Chapter (5) Healthier Alternatives

A. Baked Onion Rings with a Crunchy Quinoa Coating

Ingredients:

- 2 large onions, sliced into 1/2-inch rings
- 1 cup quinoa, cooked and cooled
- 1 cup whole wheat breadcrumbs
- 1 teaspoon garlic powder
- 1/2 teaspoon smoked paprika
- Salt and pepper, to taste
- 2 eggs, beaten
- Cooking spray

Instructions:

- **Preheat Oven:**

Preheat your oven to 425°F (220°C). Place a wire rack on a baking sheet and coat it with cooking spray.

- **Prepare Quinoa Coating:**

In a food processor, pulse the cooked quinoa until it becomes a coarse meal. Mix it with breadcrumbs, garlic powder, smoked paprika, salt, and pepper.

- **Coat in Quinoa Mixture:**

Dip each onion ring into the beaten eggs, then coat it in the quinoa mixture, pressing gently to adhere the coating.

- **Bake to Perfection:**

Place the coated onion rings on the prepared wire rack. Bake for 15-20 minutes, or until they are golden brown and crispy.

- **Serve Warm:**

Enjoy these guilt-free baked onion rings with a satisfying crunchy quinoa coating.

B. Air-Fried Onion Rings with a Light Yogurt Dip
Ingredients:

- **2 large onions, sliced into 1/2-inch rings**
- **1 cup whole wheat flour**
- **1 teaspoon garlic powder**
- **1/2 teaspoon onion powder**
- **1/2 teaspoon paprika**
- **Salt and pepper, to taste**
- **2 eggs, beaten**
- **Cooking spray**

Yogurt Dip:

- **1 cup Greek yogurt**
- **1 tablespoon lemon juice**
- **1 tablespoon chopped fresh dill**
- **Salt and pepper, to taste**

Instructions:

- **Preheat Air Fryer:**

Preheat your air fryer to 375°F (190°C).

- **Prepare Coating:**

In a bowl, combine whole wheat flour, garlic powder, onion powder, paprika, salt, and pepper.

- **Coat in Flour Mixture:**

Dip each onion ring into the beaten eggs, then coat it in the flour mixture.

- **Air Fry to Crispiness:**

Place the coated onion rings in a single layer in the air fryer basket. Spray them lightly with cooking spray. Air fry for 10-12 minutes, turning halfway through, until golden brown and crispy.

- **Prepare Yogurt Dip:**

In a small bowl, mix Greek yogurt, lemon juice, chopped dill, salt, and pepper.

- **Serve with Yogurt Dip:**

Enjoy these air-fried onion rings with a light and refreshing yogurt dip.

C. Grilled Onion Rings for a Smoky Twist
Ingredients:

- **2 large onions, sliced into 1/2-inch rings**
- **Olive oil**
- **Salt and pepper, to taste**
- **Smoked paprika, for a smoky flavor**
- **Wooden skewers, soaked in water for 30 minutes**

Instructions:

- **Preheat Grill:**

Preheat your grill to medium-high heat.

- **Prepare Onions:**

Brush each onion ring with olive oil and season with salt, pepper, and a sprinkle of smoked paprika.

- **Skewer the Rings:**

Thread the onion rings onto wooden skewers, keeping them secure and preventing them from falling through the grill grates.

- **Grill to Perfection:**

Grill the onion rings for about 3-4 minutes per side, or until they are tender and have distinct grill marks.

- **Serve Warm:**

Serve these grilled onion rings with a smoky twist as a flavorful and healthier alternative to fried versions.

Chapter (6) Dipping Sauces and Accompaniments

A. Classic Ketchup and Mayo Blend
   Ingredients:

- 1/2 cup ketchup
- 1/2 cup mayonnaise
- 1 tablespoon Dijon mustard
- 1 teaspoon Worcestershire sauce
- Salt and pepper, to taste

Instructions:

- **Combine Ingredients:**

In a bowl, whisk together ketchup, mayonnaise, Dijon mustard, and Worcestershire sauce until well combined.

- **Season to Taste:**

Add salt and pepper to taste. Adjust the quantities to achieve your preferred balance of flavors.

- **Chill and Serve:**

Refrigerate the sauce for at least 30 minutes to allow the flavors to meld. Serve alongside your favorite onion rings.

B. Tangy Sriracha Aioli
   Ingredients:

- 1/2 cup mayonnaise
- 2 tablespoons Sriracha sauce

- 1 tablespoon fresh lemon juice
- 1 clove garlic, minced
- Salt and pepper, to taste

Instructions:

- **Mix Ingredients:**

In a bowl, combine mayonnaise, Sriracha sauce, fresh lemon juice, and minced garlic.

- **Season and Blend:**

Season with salt and pepper. Stir until all ingredients are well blended.

- **Chill and Serve:**

Allow the Sriracha aioli to chill in the refrigerator for at least 15-20 minutes before serving. This tangy and spicy dip is perfect for adding a kick to your onion rings.

C. Homemade Ranch Dressing with a Kick
Ingredients:

- 1/2 cup mayonnaise
- 1/2 cup sour cream
- 2 tablespoons fresh parsley, chopped
- 1 tablespoon chives, chopped
- 1 teaspoon onion powder
- 1/2 teaspoon garlic powder
- 1/2 teaspoon smoked paprika
- Hot sauce, to taste
- Salt and pepper, to taste

Instructions:

- **Combine Ingredients:**

In a bowl, mix together mayonnaise, sour cream, chopped parsley, chopped chives, onion powder, garlic powder, and smoked paprika.

- **Add Heat:**

Add hot sauce to taste, depending on your desired level of spiciness. Stir well to incorporate.

- **Season and Chill:**

Season the ranch dressing with salt and pepper. Refrigerate for at least 1 hour before serving to allow the flavors to meld.

- **Serve with a Kick:**

This homemade ranch dressing with a kick is a flavorful accompaniment for your onion rings, adding a zesty twist to the classic ranch flavor.

Chapter (7) Tips and Tricks for Perfect Onion Rings

A. Frying Dos and Don'ts
   Dos:

- **Maintain the Right Temperature:**

Keep the oil temperature consistent. For most recipes, aim for 350°F to 375°F (175°C to 190°C).

- **Fry in Batches:**

Avoid overcrowding the fryer. Fry onion rings in small batches to ensure even cooking and crispiness.

- **Use a Slotted Spoon:**

Use a slotted spoon or tongs to carefully place and remove onion rings from the hot oil.

- **Season Immediately:**

Season the onion rings with salt or other seasonings immediately after frying while they are still hot. This helps the seasoning adhere better.

- **Drain Excess Oil:**

Place the fried onion rings on a paper towel-lined plate to absorb any excess oil.
   Don'ts:

- **Crowd the Fryer:**

Overcrowding the fryer can lead to uneven cooking and soggy onion rings. Fry in batches for optimal results.

- **Use Cold Ingredients:**

Ensure that the onions and batter ingredients are at room temperature to prevent the batter from becoming too thick.

- **Forget to Adjust Heat:**

Adjust the heat as needed. If the onion rings are browning too quickly, lower the temperature slightly.

- **Reuse Oil Too Many Times:**

While some oil reuse is acceptable, avoid using oil for too many batches, as it can affect the flavor and quality of the onion rings.

- **Underestimate Cooking Time:**

Keep a close eye on the onion rings to prevent overcooking. Remove them from the oil when they reach a golden brown color.

B. Presentation and Serving Suggestions

- **Create a Tower of Rings:**

Arrange the onion rings in a tower for an impressive and visually appealing presentation.

- **Use Different Onion Varieties:**

Experiment with different onion varieties to add visual interest and varying flavors to your presentation.

- **Serve in Cones:**

Serve individual portions in cone-shaped containers for a fun and portable presentation.

- **Garnish with Fresh Herbs:**

Garnish the plated onion rings with fresh herbs, such as parsley or chives, for a pop of color.

- **Pair with Dipping Sauces:**

Place an assortment of dipping sauces in the center of a serving platter for guests to enjoy with their onion rings.

C. Make-Ahead and Freezing Tips
Make-Ahead:

- **Prepare Sliced Onions in Advance:**

Slice the onions and store them in an airtight container in the refrigerator a day before frying.

- **Mix Dry Batter Ingredients:**

Combine the dry batter ingredients and store them in a sealed container. When ready to use, add the wet ingredients.

- **Freeze Uncooked Onion Rings:**

Freeze battered but uncooked onion rings on a baking sheet. Once frozen, transfer them to a freezer bag. Fry directly from frozen when needed.

Freezing:

- **Freeze Cooked Onion Rings:**

Allow fried onion rings to cool completely, then freeze them in a single layer on a baking sheet. Once frozen, transfer to a freezer bag.

- **Reheat in Oven or Air Fryer:**

Reheat frozen onion rings in a preheated oven or air fryer until they are crisp and heated through.

- **Avoid Freezing Dipped Rings:**

Avoid freezing onion rings that have already been dipped in sauces, as this can affect their texture when reheated.

- **Label and Date:**

Clearly label and date the freezer bags to keep track of storage times and ensure freshness.

Chapter (8) Onion Rings for Any Occasion

A. Game Day Favorites

- **Spicy Jalapeño Kick:**

Prepare a batch of spicy jalapeño onion rings for an extra kick that pairs perfectly with the excitement of game day.

- **Bacon-Wrapped Indulgence:**

Impress your game day crowd with bacon-wrapped onion rings, combining the irresistible flavors of crispy bacon and savory onions.

- **Assorted Dipping Sauces:**

Offer an array of dipping sauces, including the classic ketchup-mayo blend, tangy Sriracha aioli, and a zesty homemade ranch with a kick.

- **Serve in Stadium-Inspired Cones:**

Enhance the game day experience by serving onion rings in stadium-inspired cones for a fun and easy-to-handle snack.

B. Party Platter Perfection

- **International Flavors Platter:**

Create an onion ring platter with an international twist, featuring tempura onion rings, curried onion rings, and churro-style cinnamon sugar onion rings for a diverse and delicious spread.

- **Variety of Dipping Sauces:**

Accompany the platter with an assortment of dipping sauces, from the classic ketchup-mayo blend to the tangy Sriracha aioli and the homemade ranch with a kick.

- **Garnish with Fresh Herbs:**

Elevate the presentation by garnishing the platter with fresh herbs, adding a burst of color and freshness.

- **Serve on a Large Wooden Board:**

Arrange the onion rings on a large wooden board for a rustic and visually appealing party platter.

C. Family-Friendly Onion Ring Creations

- **Buttermilk-Soaked Southern Style Rings:**

Prepare family-friendly buttermilk-soaked Southern style onion rings for a classic and beloved flavor that's sure to please all ages.

- **Creative Shapes for Kids:**

Get creative with shapes! Cut the onions into fun shapes using cookie cutters for a kid-friendly twist on traditional rings.

- **Healthier Alternatives:**

Introduce healthier alternatives like baked onion rings with a crunchy quinoa coating, ensuring a guilt-free option for the whole family.

- **Accompany with Mild Dips:**

Pair the family-friendly onion rings with mild dipping sauces, such as the classic ketchup-mayo blend or a light yogurt dip, to suit a variety of taste preferences.

Chapter (9) Onion Rings Around the World: A Culinary Journey

A. Famous Onion Ring Destinations

- **The Varsity - Atlanta, USA:**

Experience iconic onion rings at The Varsity, a famous drive-in restaurant in Atlanta. Their colossal rings are a must-try for onion ring enthusiasts.

- **Pajo's - Steveston, Canada:**

Head to Pajo's in Steveston, known for serving crispy and golden onion rings by the waterfront. Enjoy this Canadian favorite with a view.

- **The Hand & Flowers - Marlow, UK:**

Visit The Hand & Flowers in Marlow for a Michelin-starred twist on onion rings. Here, they elevate the classic snack to gourmet heights.

B. Onion Ring Tasting Events and Festivals

- **Onion Ring Festival - Brick Lane, London:**

Attend the Onion Ring Festival in Brick Lane, London, where local vendors showcase unique and international twists on the classic onion ring.

- **International Street Food Festival - New York City, USA:**

Explore the International Street Food Festival in New York City, featuring a diverse array of onion ring variations from around the globe.

- **The Great Onion Ring Showdown - Melbourne, Australia:**

Join The Great Onion Ring Showdown in Melbourne, where chefs compete to create the most innovative and delicious onion ring creations.

C. Onion Ring Trivia and Fun Facts

- **Onion Ring Origins:**

Did you know that the exact origin of onion rings is unclear, with competing claims from different regions and time periods?

- **Largest Onion Ring:**

Learn about the world's largest onion ring, which weighed over 150 pounds and was created in 2017 in the United States.

- **Onion Rings in Pop Culture:**

Discover how onion rings have made their mark in pop culture, from being featured in classic films to becoming a viral sensation on social media.

- **Onion Rings Across Cuisines:**

Explore the ways different cultures incorporate onion rings into their cuisines, showcasing the versatility of this beloved snack around the world.

Embark on a culinary journey to discover the diverse and fascinating world of onion rings, from famous destinations to exciting events and fun facts that celebrate this globally cherished treat.

Chapter (10) Breakfast and Brunch Onion Delights

A. Onion Ring Benedict with Poached Eggs

Ingredients:

For Onion Rings:

- 2 large onions, sliced into 1/2-inch rings
- 1 cup all-purpose flour
- 1 cup buttermilk
- Salt and pepper, to taste
- Vegetable oil, for frying

For Benedict:

- 4 English muffins, split and toasted
- 8 poached eggs
- Hollandaise sauce
- Fresh chives, chopped (for garnish)

Instructions:

Prepare Onion Rings:

Follow the steps for your favorite onion ring recipe, such as the classic beer-battered or panko-crusted rings. Fry until golden brown and crispy.

Poach Eggs:

Poach the eggs using your preferred method until the whites are set and the yolks are still runny.

Assemble Benedict:

Place a generous serving of onion rings on each toasted English muffin half. Top with a poached egg.

- **Drizzle with Hollandaise:**

Spoon hollandaise sauce over the poached egg and onion rings. Garnish with chopped fresh chives.

- **Serve Warm:**

Serve immediately, and enjoy this delightful twist on Eggs Benedict with the crunchy goodness of onion rings.

B. Onion Ring Hash Browns
Ingredients:

- **2 large onions, finely chopped**
- **4 large potatoes, grated and drained**
- **1/4 cup all-purpose flour**
- **1 teaspoon garlic powder**
- **Salt and pepper, to taste**
- **Vegetable oil, for frying**

Instructions:

- **Mix Ingredients:**

In a bowl, combine finely chopped onions, grated and drained potatoes, flour, garlic powder, salt, and pepper.

- **Shape into Patties:**

Form the mixture into patties, squeezing out any excess liquid.

- **Fry to Golden Brown:**

Heat vegetable oil in a pan over medium heat. Fry the onion ring hash browns until golden brown and crispy on both sides.

- **Drain Excess Oil:**

Place the hash browns on a paper towel-lined plate to drain any excess oil.

- **Serve Hot:**

Serve these flavorful and crunchy onion ring hash browns as a delicious side for breakfast or brunch.

C. Sweet and Savory Onion Ring Pancakes
Ingredients:

- **For Onion Rings:**
- **2 large onions, sliced into 1/2-inch rings**
- **1 cup all-purpose flour**
- **1 cup buttermilk**
- **2 tablespoons sugar**
- **1 teaspoon baking powder**
- **1/2 teaspoon salt**
- **Vegetable oil, for frying**

For Pancakes:

- **1 cup all-purpose flour**
- **1 tablespoon sugar**
- **1 teaspoon baking powder**
- **1/2 teaspoon baking soda**
- **1/4 teaspoon salt**
- **1 cup buttermilk**
- **1 large egg**
- **2 tablespoons unsalted butter, melted**

Instructions:

- **Prepare Onion Rings:**

Follow the steps for your favorite onion ring recipe, incorporating a sweet element by adding sugar to the batter. Fry until golden brown and crispy.

- **Make Pancake Batter:**

In a bowl, whisk together flour, sugar, baking powder, baking soda, and salt. In a separate bowl, whisk buttermilk, egg, and melted butter. Combine the wet and dry ingredients until just mixed.

- **Fold in Onion Rings:**

Gently fold the sweet and savory onion rings into the pancake batter.

- **Cook Pancakes:**

Heat a griddle or non-stick pan over medium heat. Pour 1/4 cup portions of batter onto the griddle. Cook until bubbles form on the surface, then flip and cook until golden brown.

- **Serve Warm:**

Serve these unique sweet and savory onion ring pancakes with your favorite syrup for a delightful breakfast or brunch treat.

Chapter (11) Vegan and Gluten-Free Onion Ring Alternatives

A. Crunchy Chickpea-Crusted Onion Rings
Ingredients:

- For Onion Rings:
- 2 large onions, sliced into 1/2-inch rings
- 1 cup chickpea flour
- 1 cup sparkling water (or plain water with a pinch of baking soda)
- 1 teaspoon garlic powder
- Salt and pepper, to taste
- Vegetable oil, for frying

For Chickpea Coating:

- 1 cup chickpea breadcrumbs
- 1 teaspoon smoked paprika
- 1/2 teaspoon cumin
- Salt and pepper, to taste

Instructions:

- Prepare Onion Rings:

Slice the onions into rings and separate them.

- Make Chickpea Batter:

In a bowl, whisk together chickpea flour, sparkling water, garlic powder, salt, and pepper until smooth.

- **Prepare Chickpea Coating:**

In another bowl, combine chickpea breadcrumbs, smoked paprika, cumin, salt, and pepper.

- **Coat in Batter and Chickpea Mixture:**

Dip each onion ring into the chickpea batter, allowing excess to drip off. Coat in the chickpea breadcrumb mixture, pressing gently to adhere.

- **Fry to Golden Brown:**

Heat vegetable oil to 350°F (175°C). Fry the chickpea-crusted onion rings until golden brown and crispy, approximately 3-4 minutes per side.

- **Drain and Serve:**

Use a slotted spoon to transfer the rings to a paper towel-lined plate. Serve hot with your favorite vegan dipping sauce.

B. Gluten-Free Tempura Onion Rings
Ingredients:

- **For Onion Rings:**
- **2 large onions, sliced into 1/2-inch rings**
- **1 cup gluten-free rice flour**
- **1 cup ice-cold water**
- **Salt and pepper, to taste**
- **Vegetable oil, for frying**

Instructions:

- **Prepare Onion Rings:**

Slice the onions into rings and separate them.

- **Create Tempura Batter:**

In a bowl, whisk together gluten-free rice flour, ice-cold water, salt, and pepper until you achieve a smooth, thin batter.

- **Dip and Fry:**

Dip each onion ring into the tempura batter, coating it evenly. Fry in hot vegetable oil (350°F/175°C) until golden brown and crisp, about 2 minutes per side.

- **Drain and Serve:**

Use a slotted spoon to transfer the gluten-free tempura onion rings to a paper towel-lined plate. Serve with your favorite gluten-free dipping sauce.

C. Vegan BBQ Jackfruit-Stuffed Onion Rings
Ingredients:
For Jackfruit Filling:

- 1 can young green jackfruit, drained and shredded
- 1/2 cup vegan barbecue sauce
- 1 tablespoon olive oil
- 1 teaspoon smoked paprika
- Salt and pepper, to taste

For Onion Rings:

- 2 large onions, sliced into 1/2-inch rings
- 1 cup chickpea flour (or other gluten-free flour)
- 1 cup sparkling water (or plain water with a pinch of baking soda)
- Salt and pepper, to taste
- Vegetable oil, for frying

Instructions:

- **Prepare Jackfruit Filling:**

In a pan, heat olive oil over medium heat. Add shredded jackfruit, barbecue sauce, smoked paprika, salt, and pepper. Cook until jackfruit is tender and well-coated with sauce.

- **Prepare Onion Rings:**

Slice the onions into rings and separate them.

- **Make Chickpea Batter:**

In a bowl, whisk together chickpea flour, sparkling water, salt, and pepper until smooth.

- **Fill Onion Rings with Jackfruit:**

Take two onion rings and press them together to create a "bowl." Fill the center with the BBQ jackfruit mixture.

- **Dip and Fry:**

Dip the stuffed onion rings into the chickpea batter, coating them evenly. Fry in hot vegetable oil (350°F/175°C) until golden brown and crispy, approximately 3-4 minutes per side.

- **Drain and Serve:**

Use a slotted spoon to transfer the vegan BBQ jackfruit-stuffed onion rings to a paper towel-lined plate. Serve hot with additional barbecue sauce for dipping.

Chapter (12) Onion Ring Inspired Burgers and Sandwiches

A. The Ultimate Onion Ring Burger
Ingredients:
For Onion Rings:

- 2 large onions, sliced into 1/2-inch rings
- 1 cup all-purpose flour
- 1 cup buttermilk
- Salt and pepper, to taste
- Vegetable oil, for frying
- For Burger Patties:
- 1.5 lbs ground beef
- Salt and pepper, to taste
- Burger buns
- Lettuce, tomatoes, and other toppings of choice

Additional Toppings:

- Cheese slices
- Bacon strips
- BBQ sauce

Instructions:

- Prepare Onion Rings:

Follow the steps for your favorite onion ring recipe, such as beer-battered or panko-crusted rings. Fry until golden brown and crispy.

- Make Burger Patties:

Season the ground beef with salt and pepper. Shape into burger patties and grill to your preferred doneness.

- **Assemble the Ultimate Onion Ring Burger:**

On a toasted bun, place the grilled burger patty. Top it with cheese, crispy bacon, a generous serving of onion rings, lettuce, tomatoes, and any other toppings you desire.

- **Drizzle with BBQ Sauce:**

Drizzle the burger with your favorite BBQ sauce for an extra layer of flavor.

- **Serve Warm:**

Serve this ultimate onion ring burger hot and enjoy the combination of juicy beef, crispy onion rings, and flavorful toppings.

B. Grilled Cheese with Onion Ring Crust
Ingredients:
For Onion Rings:

- **2 large onions, sliced into 1/2-inch rings**
- **1 cup all-purpose flour**
- **1 cup buttermilk**
- **Salt and pepper, to taste**
- **Vegetable oil, for frying**

For Grilled Cheese:

- **Bread slices**
- **Butter, softened**
- **Cheese slices (cheddar, mozzarella, or your choice)**

Instructions:

- **Prepare Onion Rings:**

Follow the steps for your favorite onion ring recipe. Fry until golden brown and crispy.

- **Assemble Grilled Cheese with Onion Ring Crust:**

Butter one side of each bread slice. Place the buttered side down on a griddle or pan.

- **Add Cheese and Onion Rings:**

Add a slice of cheese to each bread slice. Place a layer of crispy onion rings on one side.

- **Form the Sandwich:**

Press the slices together to form a sandwich. Grill on both sides until the bread is golden brown, and the cheese is melted.

- **Serve Hot:**

Slice and serve this unique grilled cheese with an onion ring crust, combining the comfort of a classic grilled cheese with the crunch of onion rings.

C. Spicy Chicken and Onion Ring Sandwich
Ingredients:
For Spicy Chicken:

- **1 lb boneless, skinless chicken breasts**

- 1 cup buttermilk
- 1 cup all-purpose flour
- 1 teaspoon cayenne pepper
- Salt and pepper, to taste
- Vegetable oil, for frying

For Sandwich:

- Burger buns
- Lettuce, tomatoes, and pickles
- Spicy mayo (mayonnaise mixed with hot sauce)

Instructions:

- **Marinate Chicken:**

Marinate chicken breasts in buttermilk for at least 1 hour.

- **Prepare Spicy Chicken:**

In a bowl, mix flour, cayenne pepper, salt, and pepper. Dredge the marinated chicken in the seasoned flour mixture.

- **Fry Chicken:**

Fry the chicken in hot vegetable oil until golden brown and cooked through.

- **Prepare Onion Rings:**

Follow the steps for your favorite onion ring recipe. Fry until golden brown and crispy.
Assemble Spicy Chicken and Onion Ring Sandwich:

On a toasted bun, place the fried chicken, a layer of crispy onion rings, lettuce, tomatoes, and pickles.

- **Spread Spicy Mayo:**

Spread a generous amount of spicy mayo on the bun's top half.

- **Serve Hot:**

Serve this spicy chicken and onion ring sandwich hot for a flavorful and satisfying meal.

Chapter (13) Gourmet Onion Ring Appetizers

A. Lobster-Stuffed Onion Rings

Ingredients:

For Lobster Filling:

- 1 cup cooked lobster meat, chopped
- 2 tablespoons mayonnaise
- 1 tablespoon lemon juice
- Salt and pepper, to taste

For Onion Rings:

- 2 large onions, sliced into 1/2-inch rings
- 1 cup all-purpose flour
- 1 cup buttermilk
- Salt and pepper, to taste
- Vegetable oil, for frying

Instructions:

- **Prepare Lobster Filling:**

In a bowl, mix chopped lobster meat with mayonnaise, lemon juice, salt, and pepper. Set aside.

- **Prepare Onion Rings:**

Follow the steps for your favorite onion ring recipe, such as beer-battered or panko-crusted rings. Fry until golden brown and crispy.

- **Assemble Lobster-Stuffed Onion Rings:**

Carefully cut a slit into each fried onion ring. Stuff each ring with the lobster filling, creating a luxurious and flavorful appetizer.

- **Serve Gourmet Style:**

Arrange the lobster-stuffed onion rings on a serving platter. Garnish with additional lemon wedges and fresh herbs for a gourmet touch.

B. Truffle-Infused Onion Ring Bites
Ingredients:

- **For Truffle Aioli:**
- **1 cup vegan mayonnaise**
- **1 tablespoon truffle oil**
- **1 teaspoon lemon juice**
- **Salt and pepper, to taste**

For Onion Ring Bites:

- **2 large onions, sliced into bite-sized rings**
- **1 cup all-purpose flour**
- **1 cup buttermilk**
- **Truffle salt, to taste**
- **Vegetable oil, for frying**

Instructions:

- **Prepare Truffle Aioli:**

In a bowl, whisk together vegan mayonnaise, truffle oil, lemon juice, salt, and pepper to create a truffle-infused aioli. Set aside.

- **Prepare Onion Ring Bites:**

Follow the steps for your favorite onion ring recipe, such as beer-battered or panko-crusted bites. Fry until golden brown and crispy.

- **Season with Truffle Salt:**

While the onion ring bites are still hot, sprinkle them with truffle salt for an extra layer of gourmet flavor.

- **Serve with Truffle Aioli:**

Arrange the truffle-infused onion ring bites on a platter. Serve with the truffle aioli for dipping.

C. Foie Gras and Caramelized Onion Ring Towers
Ingredients:

- **For Foie Gras Mousse:**
- **1/2 lb foie gras, softened**
- **2 tablespoons cognac or brandy**
- **Salt and pepper, to taste**

For Caramelized Onions:

- **2 large onions, thinly sliced**
- **2 tablespoons butter**
- **1 tablespoon balsamic vinegar**
- **Salt and sugar, to taste**

For Onion Rings:

- **2 large onions, sliced into 1/2-inch rings**
- **1 cup all-purpose flour**
- **1 cup buttermilk**
- **Salt and pepper, to taste**
- **Vegetable oil, for frying**

Instructions:

- **Prepare Foie Gras Mousse:**

In a food processor, blend softened foie gras with cognac, salt, and pepper until smooth. Refrigerate until ready to use.

- **Caramelize Onions:**

In a pan, sauté thinly sliced onions in butter until soft. Add balsamic vinegar, salt, and a pinch of sugar. Continue cooking until the onions are caramelized and sweet.

- **Prepare Onion Rings:**

Follow the steps for your favorite onion ring recipe, such as beer-battered or panko-crusted rings. Fry until golden brown and crispy.

- **Assemble Towers:**

Create towers by layering foie gras mousse, caramelized onions, and crispy onion rings. Repeat the layers for a visually stunning presentation.

- **Serve Gourmet Delights:**

Serve these foie gras and caramelized onion ring towers as a gourmet appetizer for special occasions, impressing your guests with luxurious flavors and textures.

Chapter (14) Onion Rings for Dessert

A. Caramelized Onion Ring Sundae
Ingredients:
For Caramelized Onion Rings:

- 2 large onions, sliced into 1/2-inch rings
- 1 cup all-purpose flour
- 1 cup buttermilk
- Vegetable oil, for frying

For Caramel Sauce:

- 1 cup granulated sugar
- 1/4 cup water
- 1/2 cup heavy cream
- 2 tablespoons unsalted butter
- Pinch of salt

For Sundae:

- Vanilla ice cream
- Chopped nuts (optional)
- Whipped cream
- Maraschino cherries

Instructions:

- **Prepare Caramelized Onion Rings:**

Follow the steps for your favorite onion ring recipe, such as beer-battered or panko-crusted rings. Fry until golden brown and crispy.

- **Make Caramel Sauce:**

In a saucepan, combine sugar and water over medium heat. Stir until sugar dissolves, then let it cook undisturbed until it turns a deep amber color. Remove from heat and carefully add cream, butter, and a pinch of salt. Stir until smooth.

- **Coat Onion Rings in Caramel Sauce:**

Toss the warm onion rings in the caramel sauce until evenly coated.

- **Assemble Sundae:**

Place a scoop of vanilla ice cream in a bowl. Top with the caramelized onion rings. Drizzle with additional caramel sauce, add whipped cream, chopped nuts, and finish with a maraschino cherry.

- **Serve Sweet and Savory Delight:**

Enjoy this unique dessert that combines the sweetness of caramelized onion rings with the creaminess of vanilla ice cream for a delightful contrast of flavors.

B. Chocolate-Dipped Onion Rings
Ingredients:
For Chocolate-Dipped Onion Rings:

- **2 large onions, sliced into 1/2-inch rings**
- **1 cup all-purpose flour**
- **1 cup buttermilk**
- **Vegetable oil, for frying**
- **Dark chocolate, melted**

Optional Toppings:

- **Chopped nuts**
- **Shredded coconut**

- **Sprinkles**

Instructions:

- **Prepare Chocolate-Dipped Onion Rings:**

Follow the steps for your favorite onion ring recipe, such as beer-battered or panko-crusted rings. Fry until golden brown and crispy.

- **Melt Chocolate:**

Melt dark chocolate in a heatproof bowl, either over a double boiler or in the microwave, stirring until smooth.

- **Dip Onion Rings in Chocolate:**

Dip each crispy onion ring into the melted chocolate, ensuring it is well-coated. Place on a parchment-lined tray.

- **Add Optional Toppings:**

While the chocolate is still wet, sprinkle the chocolate-dipped onion rings with chopped nuts, shredded coconut, or colorful sprinkles for added texture and flavor.

- **Chill and Set:**

Allow the chocolate-dipped onion rings to chill in the refrigerator until the chocolate is fully set.

- **Serve Decadent Dessert:**

Serve these unique chocolate-dipped onion rings as a decadent dessert, surprising your taste buds with the delightful combination of savory and sweet.

C. Apple Pie-Stuffed Onion Rings
Ingredients:
For Apple Pie Filling:

- 2 apples, peeled, cored, and finely diced
- 1/4 cup brown sugar
- 1 teaspoon cinnamon
- 1/4 teaspoon nutmeg
- 1 tablespoon lemon juice

For Onion Rings:

- 2 large onions, sliced into 1/2-inch rings
- 1 cup all-purpose flour
- 1 cup buttermilk
- Vegetable oil, for frying

For Cinnamon Sugar Coating:

- 1/4 cup granulated sugar
- 1 teaspoon ground cinnamon

Instructions:

- **Prepare Apple Pie Filling:**

In a pan, combine diced apples, brown sugar, cinnamon, nutmeg, and lemon juice. Cook over medium heat until apples are tender and the mixture has a thick, syrupy consistency. Allow it to cool.

- **Prepare Onion Rings:**

Follow the steps for your favorite onion ring recipe, such as beer-battered or panko-crusted rings. Fry until golden brown and crispy.

- **Fill Onion Rings with Apple Pie Filling:**

Create a hole in the center of each fried onion ring and fill it with the cooled apple pie filling.

- **Coat in Cinnamon Sugar:**

In a bowl, mix granulated sugar and ground cinnamon. Coat the apple pie-stuffed onion rings in the cinnamon sugar mixture.

- **Serve Warm:**

Serve these delightful apple pie-stuffed onion rings warm, either on their own or with a scoop of vanilla ice cream for an indulgent dessert experience.

Chapter (15) Onion Ring Pairing: Beverages and Cocktails

A. Craft Beer and Onion Ring Pairings

1. Classic Lager and Traditional Beer-Battered Onion Rings:

- **Craft Lager Recommendation:** Crisp and clean lagers complement the savory crunch of traditional beer-battered onion rings.

2. IPA and Spicy Jalapeño Onion Rings:

- **Craft IPA Recommendation:** The hoppy and citrusy notes of an IPA contrast beautifully with the spiciness of jalapeño onion rings.

3. Stout and Bacon-Wrapped Onion Rings:

- **Craft Stout Recommendation:** Rich and robust stouts enhance the smoky flavors of bacon-wrapped onion rings, creating a hearty and satisfying pairing.

4. Wheat Beer and Parmesan Herb-infused Onion Rings:

- **Craft Wheat Beer Recommendation:** The light and refreshing character of wheat beer balances the savory and herbaceous notes of Parmesan-infused onion rings.

5. Sour Ale and Tempura Onion Rings:

- **Craft Sour Ale Recommendation:** The tartness of sour ales provides a refreshing contrast to the light and crispy texture of tempura onion rings.

B. Onion Ring Martini Mixology

1. Classic Onion Ring Martini:

Ingredients:

- **2 oz vodka**
- **1 oz dry vermouth**
- **Onion ring garnish**

Instructions:

In a mixing glass with ice, combine vodka and dry vermouth. Stir well.

Strain the mixture into a chilled martini glass.

Garnish with a small onion ring on a toothpick.

2. Spicy Jalapeño Onion Ring Margaritini:

Ingredients:

- **2 oz tequila**
- **1 oz triple sec**
- **1 oz lime juice**
- **Jalapeño-stuffed onion ring garnish**

Instructions:

Rim a martini glass with salt.

In a shaker with ice, combine tequila, triple sec, and lime juice. Shake well.

Strain into the prepared martini glass.

Garnish with a jalapeño-stuffed onion ring.

3. Sweet and Savory Caramelized Onion Martini:

Ingredients:

- **2 oz caramel vodka**

- **1 oz butterscotch schnapps**
- **Caramelized onion garnish**

Instructions:

In a shaker with ice, combine caramel vodka and butterscotch schnapps. Shake well.

Strain into a martini glass.

Garnish with a skewered caramelized onion.

C. Onion Ring-infused Milkshakes

1. Classic Vanilla Onion Ring Milkshake:

Ingredients:

- **Vanilla ice cream**
- **Milk**
- **Vanilla extract**
- **Classic onion ring crumbles**

Instructions:

In a blender, combine vanilla ice cream, milk, and a few drops of vanilla extract.

Blend until smooth.

Stir in classic onion ring crumbles.

Pour into a glass and top with additional onion ring crumbles.

2. Chocolate Hazelnut Onion Ring Shake:

Ingredients:

- **Chocolate hazelnut ice cream**
- **Hazelnut milk**
- **Chocolate syrup**
- **Chocolate-dipped onion ring garnish**

Instructions:

Blend chocolate hazelnut ice cream, hazelnut milk, and chocolate syrup until creamy.

Garnish with a chocolate-dipped onion ring on the rim of the glass.

3. Caramel Apple Pie Onion Ring Shake:

Ingredients:

- **Caramel apple pie-flavored ice cream**
- **Apple cider**
- **Caramel sauce**
- **Apple pie-stuffed onion ring garnish**

Instructions:

Blend caramel apple pie-flavored ice cream with apple cider and caramel sauce until well combined.

Garnish with an apple pie-stuffed onion ring on a straw.

Experiment with these creative pairings and mixology ideas to elevate your onion ring experience with complementary flavors and delightful beverages. Cheers to the perfect union of savory snacks and tasty drinks!

❖ Conclusion

A. Celebrating the Versatility of Onion Rings

As we wrap up this culinary journey through the world of onion rings, we celebrate the versatility of this beloved snack. From classic beer-battered rings to gourmet stuffed creations and even dessert-inspired delights, onion rings prove to be a canvas for culinary innovation. Their crispy exterior and savory flavor make them the perfect companion for various cuisines and occasions.

B. Encouragement to Create Your Own Signature Recipe

We encourage you to embrace your inner chef and embark on the adventure of creating your own signature onion ring recipe. Experiment with unique flavor combinations, diverse batters, and imaginative fillings to make onion rings truly your own. The kitchen is your playground, and the possibilities are endless.

C. Happy Frying!

As you embark on your onion ring culinary adventures, remember the joy that comes with the sizzle of onions hitting hot oil and the anticipation of that first satisfying crunch. May your onion rings be crispy, your flavors bold, and your culinary creativity boundless. Happy frying, and may your kitchen be filled with the aroma of success and deliciousness!